TSARSKOYE SELO

PALACES AND PARKS

Tsarskoye Selo had been the main residence of the imperial court, the "Russian Versailles", since the eighteenth century. The history of its creation is associated with the greatest architects – Savva Chevakinsky, Bartolomeo Francesco Rastrelli, Antonio Rinaldi, Charles Cameron and Giacomo Quarenghi.

In 2010 Tsarskoye Selo celebrated its 300th anniversary. The celebrations were centered around the world-famous palaces and parks with the pavilions recreated for the jubilee – the Concert Hall, the Turkish Bath and the Creaking Pavilion.

After many decades visitors were also given access for the first time to the Hermitage Pavilion – a unique park structure that has retained its authentic eighteenth-century decoration. As for the Catherine Palace, the recreation of its fine Arabesque Hall was finished. This interior, destroyed during the War of 1941–45, had been decorated by Cameron for Catherine the Great in keeping with the artistic tastes of the last quarter of the eighteenth century. This interior introduces visitors to the suite of Her Majesty's Own Apartments that are to be recreated in the nearest future.

The most important event of the jubilee, however, was a transfer into the possession of the museum of the Alexander Palace – the home of many generations of the Russian Emperors from which the family of the last Russian Tsar, Nicholas II, departed for their Siberian exile.

Another major event in the contemporary life of Tsarskoye Selo was the majestic ceremony of the opening of the Agate Rooms after the first stage of their restoration. The complete restoration of these uniquely magnificent interiors decorated with coloured stones of different shades, is to be carried out by 2013.

I hope that this book will serve as an introductory guide for our guests who come to the Catherine Palace and parks of Tsarskoye Selo for the first time and will also add some new glimpses for those who frequently visit our museum complex.

OLGA TARATYNOVA,
Director of the Tsarskoye Selo State Museum-Preserve

1

Tsarskoye Selo – the very name of this palace-and-park ensemble provokes a number of happy recollections. In addition to its beautiful parks and architecture, it is also associated with the great age of Russian poetry and the ceremonial glamour of the past autocratic life. In the seventeenth century, there was the Swedish farmstead *Saritsa*, later renamed *Saris hoff*, in this area. The Finnish name of the farmstead was *Saaris moisio* ("a farmstead on the elevation") and its Russianized form was *Sarskaya myza*. After Russia had eventually taken hold of these lands, Sarskaya myza (or Sarskoye Selo) became the property of Alexander Menshikov, and from 1708 to 1724 it was the summer residence of Peter the Great's wife, Yekaterina Alexeyevna (future Catherine I). In 1711, after she was declared "the true Sovereign", the building of a large-scale residence began on the site. Johann Braunstein and Johann Christian Förster were mainly responsible for its construction.

Catherine I bequathed Sarskoye Selo to her daughter, Tsarevna Elizabeth Petrovna. On becoming the Empress in 1741, she, with her innate breadth of nature, did not spare funds for turning the old mansion into a luxurious palace, for building various pavilions and for laying-out gardens. In 1743–51 the Empress's projects for the extension of the suburban residence were carried out by Mikhail Zemtsov, Alexei Kvasov and Savva Chevakinsky. In 1752–56, the work on the estate, by then already renamed Tsarskoye Selo, or the Tsars' Village, was supervised by Bartolomeo Francesco Rastrelli. It was he who gave to the palace and the entire complex that luxurious Baroque appearance which was poetically compared with a "celestial constellation". It was only during the reign of Elizabeth, and through the efforts of Rastrelli, who believed that palaces should be created "for the common glory of Russia", that this residence could rightfully be called – the Tsar's Village.

In 1744, Elizabeth Petrovna commissioned Rastrelli to build "a palace with truly splendid ornaments, fit to be an abode for the ruler of a huge empire". "At first, while the palace was under construction, the ornaments gleamed,

1. Friedrich Hartmann Barisien.
View of the Great Palace and Sadovaya Street at Tsarskoye Selo. 1760

2. Mikhail Makhayev.
Panoramic View of the Great (Catherine) Palace.
Mid-18th century

2

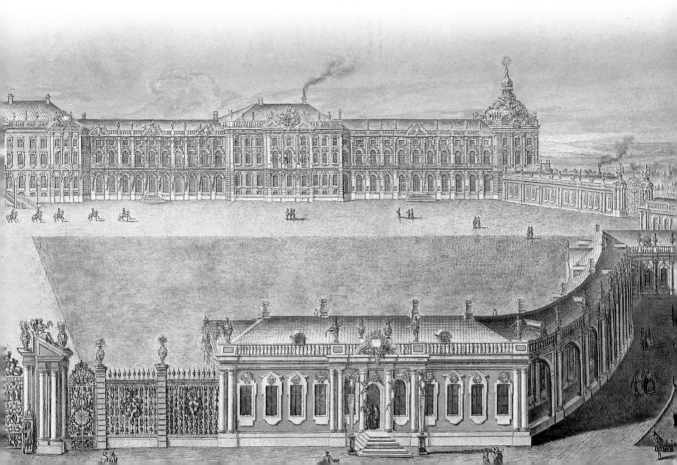

3

4

5

and when Empress Elizabeth arrived to view it in the company of her entire court and the foreign ministers, they were all stunned by its splendour, and each of the courtiers rushed to express his amazement" (Mikhail Pyliayev).

A group of actors, under the direction of the son of the Yaroslavl merchant Fiodor Volkov, made its first appearance before a royal audience in the Catherine Palace. Empress Elizabeth, who had heard a great deal about the talents of the young actors, wished to witness them for herself. Delighted by what she saw, Elizabeth invited Volkov and his associates to Petersburg, and in 1756 she issued a decree on the founding of the Russian professional theatre.

Later on, Empress Catherine II devoted much time and care to the development of the estate and "here her genius and fine taste were revealed". During the reign of Catherine the Great Tsarskoye Selo was further enriched with the works of the architects Antonio Rinaldi, Yury

Velten, Vasily Neyelov, Charles Cameron and Giacomo Quarenghi, whose tastes were formed under the influence of ancient architecture.

The Alexander Palace was built by Catherine the Great as a gift to her first and favourite grandson Alexander Pavlovich (the future Alexander I) on the occasion of his wedding to Grand Duchess Elizabeth Alexeyevna, née the Baden Princess Luise-Marie-Augusta. Carrying out the imperial commission, Giacomo Quarenghi created in 1792–96 one of the most perfect landmarks of world architecture the significance of which is not subject to the influence of time. This delightful building is the architectural and aesthetic centrepiece of the Alexander Park. The palace's façades are very simple. They are adorned with colonnade comprising double rows of Corinthian columns.

3. Benoît Coffre. *Portrait of Peter the Great*.
First quarter of the 18th century

4. Ivan Adolsky. *Portrait of Empress Catherine I*. 1726

5. Heinrich Buchgolz. *Portrait of Empress Elizabeth Petrovna*. 1760s

6. Mikhail Ivanov. *The Great Pond. View of the Chesme Column.*
1790s. Watercolour

7. Vladimir Borovikovsky.
Catherine the Great on a Stroll in the Tsarskoye Selo Park

8

9

10

11

8. Valerian Languer. *The Great Pond.
View of the Chesme Column*. 1820. Watercolour

9. Anonymous artist. *Emperor Alexander I
with the Grand Dukes Nicholas Pavlovich
and Konstantin Pavlovich*. Early 19th century

10. George Dawe. *Empress Yelizaveta Alexeyevna
at Tsarskoye Selo*. Not later than 1825

11. Timoleon von Neff.
Grand Duchesses Maria and Olga. 1838

12. Horace Vernet. *Knight Tournament in Tsarskoye Selo.
Empress Alexandra Fiodorovna and Emperor Nicholas I
Dressed in Mediaeval Suits*. 1842

13. Valerian Languer. *The Great Pond.
The Cameron Gallery and the Grotto*. 1820. Engraving

→

14. Vasily Sadovnikov. *Façade of the Great Palace
at Tsarskoye Selo (view from the main square)*

12

13

15

16

17

Catherine the Great personally oversaw the education of Alexander I, Paul's eldest son, and patronised him in a number of ways. The Empress wanted to make him her heir in order to deprive Paul, whom she disliked, of his right to the throne and thus vex her son even from beyond the grave. Although Alexander I almost did not live in the palace on his accession to the throne, this great creation by Quarenghi bears his name.

When Alexander I became Emperor after the assassination of his father, which was committed with Alexander's mute consent, the palace was given to the future tsar, Grand Duke Nicholas. Alexander III also lived there prior to his ascension to the throne, and Nicholas II chose the palace as his permanent residence. The Alexander Palace became the last refuge of the royal family after Nicholas II was deposed in March 1917. From here, he and his family were taken to Tobolsk and then to Ekaterinburg, where they were executed in July 1918.

15. Konstantin Ukhtomsky. *The Bedchamber of the Empress Elizabeth Alexeyevna*. Mid-19th century. Watercolour

16. Luigi Premazzi. *The Picture Hall*. 1870. Watercolour

17. Luigi Premazzi. *The Great Hall of the Agate Rooms*. Mid-19th century. Watercolour

18. Eduard Gau. *The Arabesque Room in the Great Palace of Tsarskoye Selo*. 1850. Watercolour

19. Friedrich Hartmann Barisien. *View of the Great Palace of Tsarskoye Selo*. 1760. Watercolour

20. Alexander Kolb. *The Third Anteroom in the Great Palace of Tsarskoye Selo*. 1865. Watercolour

18

23

←
21, 22. The Catherine Palace (1752–56, architect: Bartolomeo
Francesco Rastrelli, sculptor: Johann Franz Duncker). The garden front

23, 24. The Catherine Palace. Moulded decoration of the façade

25. The Catherine Palace. The main porch of the garden front

24

25

26, 27. The Catherine Palace.
View of the façade from the main courtyard

28. The Catherine Palace.
Cartouche with the crown and monogram of Catherine I on the main pediment of the Middle House

29. The Catherine Palace.
View of the façade from the main courtyard. Portico. Statue: *Glory*. Early 18th century. Venice. Marble

30. The Catherine Palace. View of the façade from the main courtyard. Portico

26

29

30

THE CATHERINE PALACE

It is the Catherine Palace the fronts of which extend for 740 metres, that dominates the entire complex of Tsarskoye Selo. Rastrelli not only completely altered the dimensions of the latter, but also adorned them with lavish sculptural designs inside and out. The palace's external ornaments give a highly accurate impression of the creativeness and imagination of the architect, who succeeded in endowing the 300-metre-long façade with a plastic expressiveness. No expense was spared on this building: 100 kilograms of gold alone were used for the decorations.

31. A bird's-eye view of the Catherine Palace and the parterre

32. The Catherine Palace. The garden front

33. The Catherine Palace. Moulded decoration of the façade

34

35

THE MAIN STAIRCASE

The impression of the palace's truly imperial magnificence is enhanced by its interiors, the decor of which reflects the rapidly changing tastes of their crowned owners. This change can be observed in the design of the imperial apartments where Baroque luxury neighbours with Classical elegance.

The famous marble Main Staircase by Hippolyto Monighetti, is striking for the monumental character of its design. The staircase with two tiers of windows overlooking the Catherine and Alexander Parks occupies a special place in the composition of the Catherine Palace. It is from this interior that the overall conception of the palace and park ensemble can be most clearly perceived.

The Main Staircase is designed in the style that makes it comparable to Rastrelli's interiors. The rocaille moulded ornamentation of the walls and ceilings, the paintings by Italian painters of the seventeenth and eighteenth centuries adorning the ceiling, the pieces of marble sculpture (*Sleeping Cupid* and *Awakening Cupid*) on the landings, the Japanese and Chinese porcelain on the wall consoles, all makes this palatial staircase particularly impressive.

38

39

THE GREAT HALL

The Great Hall (or the Ballroom) is a true master-piece of the decorative genius of Bartolomeo Francesco Rastrelli. This is one of the largest palatial halls created by this outstanding architect in St Petersburg and its environs in the 1750s.

The hall's area is 846 square metres (it is seventeen metres wide and forty-seven metres long). Bright and airy, the room seems even larger than it actually is because of the many mirrors, the abundance of gilding and, in particular, the spectacular painted ceiling, which creates an illusion of endless space.

Rastrelli wanted the room to be perceived as an integral whole, so he concealed the stoves necessary to heat this huge hall behind false windows with mirrored glass. The impression of its great expanse is still further enhanced thanks to the illusion of space created by the two tiers of windows.

The main element in the decoration of the Great Hall is gilded carving. The endless figures and half-figures – putti and "seated ladies", interlacing orna-ments, whimsical cartouches and rocailles strike us

38. Detail of the interior

39. The western wall

40. Detail of the ceiling painting *The Triumph of Russia*

41. The Great Hall

→

42. The ceiling painting *The Triumph of Russia*

by their exceedingly imaginative and still realistic treatment. During the restoration of the Great Hall some parts of the carved work were restored and some others were recreated from similar examples in accordance with the techniques of woodwork employed in the eighteenth century.

The grandiose ceiling painting *The Triumph of Russia* and the fanciful pattern of the inlaid parquetry enhance the decorative effect of the Great Hall. The elaborate pictorial composition of *The Triumph of Russia* in the centre of the ceiling consists of three pictures executed by Giuseppe Valeriani, an eminent master of decorative painting. The parquet floor with star-shaped diverging rays made after Rastrelli's sketch from the woods available in Russia – light and tinted oak, maple and walnut – was restored.

46

43–46. Details of carved decoration

Nevertheless the predominant decorative element of the interior is gilded carving. Countless figures and half-figures, ornamental interlaces, cartouches and rocailles produce an indelible impression on visitors by their fantastic ingenuity and mastery of their execution.

→

47. View of the Main Courtyard

→

48. Entrance to the First Anteroom

49

THE FIRST ANTEROOM

Glazed doors lead from the Great Hall to three Anterooms adorned with lavish gilded carving from Rastrelli's sketches characteristic of the Baroque style. The architect designed five Anterooms, but the last two have not reached us. In the 1780s Charles Cameron rebuilt them into the Lyon and Arabesque Halls. Located directly in front of the Great Hall, the First Anteroom is remarkable for its large dimensions and abundance of carved and gilded decoration. Carving covered its walls all over, the divided pilasters with capitals in the form of triglyphs were situated over the upper and lower windows; the carved figures of seated women and cupids embellished the over-door pediments. 330 candles set in girandoles illuminated the hall. In 1765, for Catherine's birthday, in the First Anteroom was arranged a theatre and since then court performances and small-scale balls were held in the Anteroom every year. The ceiling painting *Bacchus and Ariadne* was a work by the Italian artists Pietro and Francesco Gradizzi.

49. The First Anteroom

50. Detail of the top of a tile stove

51. View of the ceiling painting *Bacchus and Ariadne*

52, 53. Details of the ceiling painting *Bacchus and Ariadne*

50

28

51

52

53

THE SECOND ANTEROOM

The walls of the Second Anteroom are adorned with carved designs. The main decorative elements here are pilasters with diverse carved ornaments and mirrors in sumptuous gilded frames over the fireplaces. 270 candles, reflecting in the mirror surface, create additional light effects. The artist Fedot Kolokolnikov produced the ceiling painting Bacchus and Ariadne from a sketch by Antonio Peresinotti. The ornate frame of this picture contained coats-of-arms, cupids and rocaille arabesques. For a long time in this Anteroom stood a wooden cabinet and a gymnastic turnstile, intended for games and amusements of the children of the imperial family.

54, 55. The Second Anteroom.
Details of the carved decoration

56. The Second Anteroom.
View of the Agate Rooms Pavilion

54

55

56

57

58

THE THIRD ANTEROOM

Rastrelli based the principal decorative accent in the Third Anteroom on the combination of gilded carving with blue tones of the ceiling painting Olympus. Contemporaries regarded it as "the most beautiful from the three Elizabethan ceiling paintings". Its authorship is ascribed to the artists Antonio Peresinotti, Pietro Gradizzi and Ivan Belsky. In the Third Anteroom theatrical performances were also sometimes held, which is confirmed by the presence of a stage here. In the reign of Catherine the Great in the Anteroom was installed a table for the game of billiards that became fashionable in the 1760s.

57. The Second Anteroom

58. The Second Anteroom. Detail of the ceiling painting *Bacchus and Ariadne*

31

59

60

Alexander II, who had a liking for it, ordered in 1845 to dismantle the stage that restrained players' movements.

Restoration work in the Anterooms began with the re-creation of the ceiling paintings lost during the War of 1941–45. In 1985, using pre-war photographs and nineteenth-century watercolours, restorers managed to produce a copy of the ceiling painting in the Third Anteroom. The ceiling painting of the Second Anteroom was completed in 1991 taking as a model the fresco The Apotheosis of Bacchus by Jacopo Guarano, who was active in the Winter Palace. By December 1999 was painted anew from surviving photographs the ceiling painting of the First Anteroom. The work, enormous in scale and complexity, was carried out by well-known artists-restorers, State Prize Winners I. Alexeyev, B. Lebedev, Ya. Kazakov and Yu. Shitov. Their creative work was connected with the revival of monumental painting in the palace and park ensemble of Tsarskoye Selo for several decades.

59. The Third Antechamber

60. Detail of the ceiling painting *Olympus*

61, 62. Details of the carved decoration

61

62

63

64

63. The Arabesque Hall

64. The moulded decoration of the wall

65–67. Details of the painted decoration of the cornice

68. Ceiling painting

THE ARABESQUE HALL

The Arabesque Hall (133.9 square metres in area, 14.3 m long and 9.3 m wide) is one of the most impressive state rooms in the private apartments of Catherine the Great. It was in this hall that majestic ceremonies were usually held during the Empress's summer sojourns at Tsarskoye Selo and it was also here that Catherine preferred to spend evening hours playing cards. The two doors of this hall that replaced the Fourth Anteroom, connect it along the axis of the suite with the Third Anteroom and the Lyon Hall (now under restoration); the windows (four above and two below) overlook the main square.

Charles Cameron began to work on the project of the Arabesque Hall soon after his arrival at Tsarskoye Selo, in 1781, and completed it in 1784. This interior, designed in the style of Early Classicism, appears light and majestic thanks to its white-blue and golden colour scheme and two-tiered architectural solution (the two-partite articulation of the hall emphasizes the moulded cornice running along the entire perimeter and separating the upper part of the walls from the lower section). The artistic image of the Arabesque Hall is determined by the rhythmic arrangement of the elegant fluted pilasters that emphasize the slender architectonics of the interior, to which the entire decorative design is subordinated. Its main materials are wood, bronze and plaster of Paris, and its techniques combine carving, moulding, gilding and chasing, as well as oil painting and painting on stucco. The hall owes its name to the elegant ornaments of the ceiling painting and the arabesque motifs in the decoration of the walls.

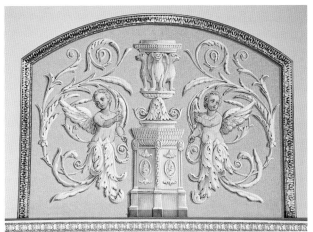

65

66

67

68

THE DINING ROOM FOR CAVALIERS-IN-ATTENDANCE

Along with majestic ceremonies the palace was the venue of more intimate receptions to which only guests belonging to a narrow circle were invited. Next to the Great Hall is the Dining Room for Cavaliers-in-Attendance where parties of this sort were held. This Dining Room is remarkable for its golden decor shining in numerous mirrors as well as for the painted insets of hunting scenes in round frames over the mirrors as well as for the fine table appointments and decoration. It is interesting that in the middle of the eighteenth century the tables were not standing here permanently but were brought in only for dinners.

The ceiling painting by an anonymous Russian painter of the mid-eighteenth century is devoted to a subject from ancient Greek mythology. It features Helios, the sun god, and Eos, the goddess of the dawn, surrounded by the allegories of seasons.

69. Detail of the interior

70. The Dining Room for Cavaliers-in-Attendance

71. Items from the St George Order Service. 1780s.
F. Gardner Factory, Russia. Porcelain

72

73

74

75

THE WHITE DINING ROOM

Symmetrically to the Dining Room for Cavaliers-in-Attendance, to the north of the Main Staircase, is the White Dining Room, followed by the Portrait Hall showing large representative portraits of the Empresses Catherine I and Elizabeth. In the eighteenth century, the age of amusements and festivities, a great significance was attached to the laying and decoration of tables. The feasts held in the White Dining Room were especially sumptuous. The table, shaped like the E monogram, was skilfully draped by a snow-white cloth adorned with garlands of flowers. It was set with the so-called Her Majesty's Own Service produced at the celebrated Fiodor Gardner Porcelain Factory. The walls of the Dining Room are embellished with paintings by the court artist Johann Friedrich Grooth featuring hunting scenes.

77

72. Johann Friedrich Grooth. *Storks.* 1757

73. Table decoration. 1760s. Imperial Porcelain Factory, St Petersburg

74. Centrepiece, an ornament placed on a table during the dining parties in the 18th century

75. Johann Friedrich Grooth. *Owl on a Bough.* 1750s

76. The White Dining Room

77. Glass objects. 1830s. Imperial Glass Works, St Petersburg

78

THE CRIMSON AND GREEN PILASTER DRAWING ROOMS

The Golden Suite unites into a single whole a series of ornate interiors running along the first floor of the Catherine Palace. The walls and window surrounds in these departments are trimmed with gilded carvings forming rocaille ornamental and figure compositions; the ceiling is embellished with stuccowork shining with gold and paintings; the floor is decorated with inlaid parquetry. The white damask, which is used to upholster the walls of the rooms, has been woven on special looms after eighteenth-century original examples. All the rooms of this state enfilade contain stoves with niches and fancy-shaped cornices decorated with cobalt painting in imitation of tiles.

78. The Crimson Pilaster Drawing Room.
Ceiling painting *Alexander the Great and the family of the Persian Shah Darius*

79. Secretary. 18th century. By Abraham Roentgen, Germany

80. The Golden Enfilade.
View from the Crimson Pilaster Drawing Room

→
81. The Crimson Pilaster Drawing Room

79

82. The Green Pilaster Drawing Room

83. The Green Pilaster Drawing Room. Ceiling painting *Resting Army Commander Listening to the Voice of the Muses*

84. The Crimson Pilaster Drawing Room. Standard lamp shaped like the figure of a Negro. Mid-18th century. Western Europe (Italy?). Panel

The Crimson and Green Pilaster Drawing Rooms following the White State Dining Room have an unusual and impressive appearance. They owe much of their unusual look to the pilasters rhythmically articulating the walls. These are made of glass with brightly coloured foil put under it, so that the texture of the foil is reminiscent of a play of gems. Framed by gilded carving, these pilasters look highly ornate. The Crimson and Green Drawing Rooms are decorated with ceiling paintings. In the eighteenth century they had no special designation.

Nowadays the exhibition displayed in these rooms emphasizes its playing character. The card table in the centre of the room bears China-made chess carved in ivory, with mother-of-pearl insets.

An indispensable attribute in all the interiors of the Catherine Palace created by Rastrelli was a tall hexagonal stove faced with tiles painted in cobalt blue. Such stoves can be seen in the Crimson and Green Pilaster Drawing Rooms, too.

84

86

THE PORTRAIT HALL

The images of the Emperors and the Empresses of the Romanov Dynasty, whose names are associated with the history of the Catherine Palace, occupy an important place in its collection of painting. In the Portrait Hall one can see the well-known portrait of Catherine I by Ivan Adolsky, which shows her in a formal dress, with the band of St Andrew the First-Called.

Catherine could hardly be called a beauty, but in her "burning eyes, in her scarlet lips and round chin, and in her face in general, was so much burning passion…, that it is not difficult to understand how such colossus as Peter gave himself wholly to 'this hearty friend'."

Displayed in the same hall is a portrait of Elizabeth Petrovna, daughter of Peter the Great and Catherine I, a painting by the German painter Heinrich Buchholz, created in the 1760s, i.e. already after the death of the Empress. The palaces erected by Russian architects for her in St Petersburg and in its environs struck contemporaries by their glitter and luxury and the Empress herself, a stately blonde, personified the type of a real Russian beauty. In keeping with the demands of formal portrait portraiture, the artist created an idealized and generalized image of the Empress. The carefully painted draperies, the rich fabrics of her costume, its accessories and ermine fur lend to Elizabeth's likeness a required dignified and impressive appearance. The first women who owned the palace are represented with all their imperial regalia. The Tsarinas' crowns, sceptres and orbs in their hands, made by the best jewellers of the period, are notable examples of art. Today these symbols of regal power are preserved in Moscow, at the State Armoury.

Hanging in the hall are also the portraits of Natalia Alexeyevna, sister of Peter the Great, and the German Princess Auguste Sophie Friederike of Anhalt-Zerbst (Catherine II), who dethroned her consort, Peter III, in 1762, was proclaimed Empress of Russia and ruled Russia successfully for 34 years. The portraits are copies from the originals by Ivan Nikitin and Fiodor Rokotov correspondingly.

85. The Portrait Hall

86. Ceiling painting *Mercury and Glory*

87, 88. Decoration of the upper section of the doorway

87

88

THE AMBER ROOM

Powerful Baroque forms determine the plastic expressiveness of the palace endowing it with a truly regal majesty. This impression is enhanced by the interiors of the palace the decor of which reflects the swiftly changing tastes of the crowned owners. They are recorded in the decorative styles of the rooms and halls.

A veritable gem of the Catherine Palace was the Amber Study which is justly ranked by connoisseurs among "treasures of the world".

In 1701–09 Gottfried Wolfram, Gottfried Turau and Ernst Schacht produced, after a design by Andreas Schlüter, the inlaid amber

89. Frederick I's coat of arms. Amber. Detail of the lower frieze decor

90. Clock decorated with porcelain flowers.
Mid-18th century. Bronze, porcelain. Workshop of G. Cosar, France

91. Detail of the carved wooden decoration of the cornice
→
92. The north-western section
→
93. The western wall
→
94. Panorama of the Amber Room

panels which in 1717 were sent by the Prussian king, Frederick William I, to Peter the Great as a gift for the decoration of the Study in his Winter Palace at St Petersburg. In 1755 Rastrelli designed the Amber Room in the Catherine Palace enriching the panels with Florentine mosaics and sculpture. The unpanelled area of the walls was skilfully decorated with mirrors, murals and gilded wood-carving.

Anyone who ever saw the Amber Room was enchanted by it. One French author wrote about this room: "The eye, unused to seeing amber in such quantities, is captivated and blinded by the wealth and warmth of the tones, which encompass every shade of yellow, from dusky topaz to bright lemon…"

During the Second World War, almost all amber objects were removed to Novosibirsk, but the panels of the Amber Room were looted by the Nazi soldiers. The current exhibition is comprised of the works that were saved or restored. The mosaics lining the walls are being recreated by contemporary craftsmen. Fortunately, the room has nowadays completely regained its former splendour.

95. View of the ceiling painting *The Wedding of Saturn* and the upper tier of the walls

96. Mirror cartouche in a carved amber frame with the imperial crown

97. Mask in the upper section of the amber panel

102

103

104

105

106

107

←
98. Mosaic picture *The Senses of Touch and Smell* on the southern wall

←
99. Mosaic picture *The Sense of Hearing* on the eastern wall

←
100. Mosaic picture *The Sense of Eyesight* on the northern wall

←
101. Mosaic picture *The Sense of Taste* on the eastern wall

102. Casket. Second half of the 17th century.
Circle of M. Redlin, Gdansk. Amber, wood, metal and velvet

103. Casket. 1705.
By Gottfried Turau, Germany. Amber, wood and metal

104. The southern wall

105. Detail of the decoration of the cornice and ceiling cove

106. Detail of the Large Amber Frame on the southern wall

107. Chess and trick-track. Early 18th century. Workshop of
G. Schreiber (?), Königsberg. Amber, wood, ivory, mastic and metal

THE PICTURE HALL

The Picture Hall, an interior the decor of which is largely devoted to painting, is characteristic of the first half of the eighteenth century. The powerful decorative effect created by tapestry-like hanging of the canvases combines here with the image of a picture gallery, an indispensable attribute in the home of an enlightened aristocrat during that period.

Rastrelli completely covered the longitudinal walls with 130 paintings by Luca Giordano, Emmanuel de Witte, Adriaen van Ostade, David Teniers and other eminent Western European artists of the seventeenth and eighteenth centuries. Two paintings, *The Battle of Poltava* and *The Battle of Lesnaya*, were commissioned by Peter the Great from the French painter Pierre Denis Martin.

108. The Picture Hall

109. Detail of the inlaid parquet floor

110. The Golden Suite.
View from the Picture Hall

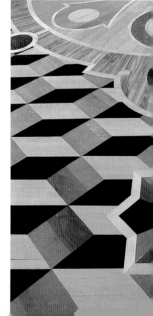

109

110

55

111

112

113

111. Pierre Denis Martin the Younger. *The Battle of Poltava*. 1717

112. Jean Baptiste Nattier the Elder. *An Allegory of Sculpture*. 1715

113. Unknown 17th-century Flemish artist. *Flowers n a Vase*

114. Jan van Huysum. *The Magnanimity of Scipio Africanus*

115. Henri Blanchard. *Jupiter and Danaë*. 1829 (?)

114

115

THE SMALL WHITE DINING ROOM
THE DRAWING ROOM OF ALEXANDER I

The interiors behind the Picture Hall continued Rastrelli's enfilade and although in the early nineteenth century they were rearranged as the private apartments of Alexander I, the decoration of the middle of the eighteenth century was left intact.

The Picture Hall adjoins the Small White Dining Room. Its walls are upholstered with white damask. The doors are adorned with carved and gilded over-door decorations executed from models by the sculptor Johann Franz Duncker. Each of them is a composition consisting of a cartouche, hunting trumpets, a quiver, an eagle with its wings flung open, shells and garlands with flowers.

On the walls of the Drawing Room of Alexander I hang portraits of Catherine I, Peter the Great, Elizabeth Petrovna and Anna Ioannovna painted by the court painter Louis Caravaque, a portrait of Catherine II – a copy done by an unknown painter of the second half of the eighteenth century from the original by Johann-Baptist Lampi the Elder – and a portrait of Alexander I by George Dawe. The ceiling painting is a replica of the painting *Venus in a Chariot* by François Boucher. It was painted by the artists-restorers V. Zhuravliov and A. Snetkov in the 1970s.

116, 119. The Small White Dining Room

117. The Drawing Room of Alexander I

118. The Drawing Room of Alexander I. Ceiling painting *Venus in a Chariot*

121

THE GREEN DINING ROOM

The Green Dining Room, decorated after drawings by Cameron, represents a version of the subtle interpretation of ancient motifs in the Russian interiors of the 1780s. Cameron freely improvised on the subject of ancient Roman decorative motifs. He attained the harmony of his artistic solution primarily by the use of plastic elements. The moulded details are arranged against the light green background of the walls with a thorough calculation. The main field is enlivened by a stylized representation of garden gates with medallions and moulded figures of youths and girls, seemingly supporting bas-reliefs with scenes of playing Cupids. The crowning element of the wall composition are arc-shaped twigs of vine. The delicate tracery of details and the jeweller's modelling of sculptural forms executed by Ivan Martos after Cameron's drawings lend the Green Dining Room that sense of elegance which dominates the living apartments of the Catherine Palace.

120. Fireplace. 1780s. Designed by Charles Cameron

121. The Green Dining Room

122. Clock. Second half of the 18th century. France. Bronze, marble

THE WAITERS' ROOM

The Waiters' Room is one of service rooms of the palace where in the eighteenth century tables for dinners held in the Green Dining Room were served. The interior designed by Cameron was divided by a transverse screen into two "entrance rooms", one of which faced the staircase. After a fire of 1820 the decoration of the Waiters' Room was restored by Vasily Stasov. The architect preserved the symmetrical articulation of the interior by wooden pilasters painted in imitation of marble and linked by plaster arches. In the 1840s Stasov removed the partition by a decree of Emperor Nicholas I and the two "entrance rooms" turned into a spacious light room. In 1959 hall was repaired with a re-creation of details from Stasov's drawings as Cameron's projects have not survived.

123, 125. The Waiters' Room

124. Bartolomé Esteban Murillo. *Mountain Landscape*
(Landscape Decorated by a Moorish Structure on the Mountain)

124

THE MAIN BLUE DRAWING ROOM

The Main Blue Drawing Room, the central apartment of the north section of the palace, is one of the most remarkable interiors in the palace created by Cameron in the 1780s. Notable features of this interior are the silk upholstery of its walls adorned with a printed pattern, the artistic paintings of the ceilings and doors as well as the inlaid parquet floor. In all this majestic spectacle free improvisations of motifs borrowed from

128

ancient art can be traced. Set into the moulded frieze with a gilded relief ornament are painted medallions featuring ancient images. The ceiling of the Main Blue Drawing Room is embellished with decorative painting based on semi-circles, rectangles and squares. Painted within the geometrical figures are mythological scenes and characters. The rich design of the inlaid parquet floor matches the elaborate compositional forms of the painted ceiling. Cameron especially loved to use unusual combinations of painting, gilding, decorative fabrics and items of furniture in his interiors. In the Main Blue Drawing

Room, for example, pale blue silk with a flower print serves as a delightful backdrop for the austere Classical forms of the furniture and mirrors. The standard lamps made of blue glass and positioned in the corners of the room make a delightful addition to its decorative fittings. In Cameron's day, fireplaces for heating the vast rooms first appeared in the palace chambers and were constructed precisely according to his designs.

126, 128. The Main Blue Drawing Room

127. Clock: *Bacchus*. 18th century. France. Gilded bronze

127

129

129. Detail of the upholstery

130. Decorative statuettes: *Chinese Man*
and *Chinese Woman*. China. Porcelain

131. The Chinese Blue Drawing Room

132. The central part of the ceiling painting

130

THE CHINESE BLUE DRAWING ROOM

The Chinese Blue Drawing Room is otherwise known as the Main Study. The silks and porcelain fittings used in the decor of this chamber were brought to Russia in the mid-eighteenth century when trade links with China began to develop. Its walls are lined from top to bottom with blue silk which is embellished with stylized scenes of "Chinese life" painted in varicoloured inks.

It is remarkable that Cameron, a convinced Classicist, combined the *chinoiserie* upholstery of the walls with ancient motifs of the ceiling painting, which lent the interior an air of artistic originality. The silk used for lining the walls in the reign of Catherine the Great was brought from China, but it was destroyed during the Second World War. The lost fabrics were recreated by restorers on the basis of a surviving sample.

134

THE CHOIR ANTEROOM

The Choir Anteroom is an interior in the northern half of the palace that Empress Catherine allotted to Grand Duke Pavel Petrovich, the heir to the throne, and his wife, Grand Duchess Maria Fiodorovna. The Choir Anteroom owes its name to its location near the choir of the home church. As is known, Catherine invited the Scottish architect Charles Cameron to design the interior. However, the stylistic elements typical of this outstanding exponent of Classicism can hardly be discerned in the decor of the Choir Anteroom, because it has been repeatedly altered.

The distinctive feature of this interior is the trimming of its walls with silk bearing woven varicoloured depictions of swans and pheasants. The fabric was produced by Russian weavers from a sketch made in France for the Lyons Factory. The silk is authentic and therefore very rare – during the war the staff members succeeded to evacuate it to the hinterland.

The gilded eighteenth-century set of furniture installed in the Choir Anteroom was made after a drawing by Rastrelli and later upholstered with a nineteenth-century silk. The decor of the Choir Anteroom lends to this interior, modest in dimensions, the majesty of a true state room.

133. Detail of the upholstery

134. The Choir Anteroom

135. Candelabrum. Mid-18th century. France. Bronze

135

136

THE BEDROOM

During the reign of Catherine the Great, new interiors appeared in the palace, associated with Cameron. The use of subtly adapted forms derived from Greco-Roman decor is characteristic of the works of this outstanding master of Classicism. Catherine the Great commissioned Cameron the designing of the heir's apartments, and Cameron brilliantly coped with the task.

The Bedroom of Maria Fiodorovna is one of the most spectacular interiors created by Cameron in the Catherine Palace. This is the largest of Paul I and Maria Fiodorovna's private rooms. The architectural image of this room combined the intimate character of a private apartment with the luxury of a state room. Elegant alcoves and refined decorations lend the chamber a special charm. Cameron used for the decor of the Bedroom moulded wall panels executed by Ivan Martos, which allegorically personified joy and happiness of family life.

The most prominent feature of the Bedroom are slender faience columns of the alcove. Lavishly ornamented and emphasized by gilded strips and flutes, they are entwined with garlands. Arranged with a subtle sense of rhythm, the stucco frieze against the pale green walls, and the delicately gilded mouldings are all reminiscent of the features of the famous Pompeiian villas' murals.

136. The Bedroom

137. Door decoration

138. *Cupid.* Second half of the 18th century, sculptor: N. Gillée. Marble

137

139

THE STUDY FOR PAINTING
THE STUDY FOR CARVING

The Bedchamber adjoins the small-size Study for Painting (Pale Yellow Divan Room) and the Study for Carving (or Sculpture). They were intended correspondingly for painting and ivory carving – hence their names. Created in the in 1780s by Cameron, the Study was re-designed by Vasily Stasov after a fire of 1820. At the present time they were restored to their pre-war appearance.

In the first Study the walls have a historical golden-yellow colouring. From the late eighteenth century have survived a framing frieze and a cornice of gilded moulding; from the same period dates the decoration of the doors. The painting of the cross vault, lunette and frieze was created anew after the fire by Dmitry Antonelli, an Academician of Painting. The furniture was made of maple in the nineteenth century in the workshop of A. Tour and painted by the

139. The Study for Painting
(Pale Yellow Sofa Room). Harp from Great Britain. First quarter of the 19th century. S. Erar Factory, London. Wood and brass

140. The Study for Painting
(Pale Yellow Sofa Room).
P.-Ch. Tremollière. *Spring (Zephyr)*

141. The Study for Carving (or Sculpture)

artist Giuseppe Bernasconi. On the table stands a "miracle" candlestick made of bronze and mother-of-pearl by a French craftsman in the first half of the nineteenth century.

In the Study for Sculpture prevail relief decorations of a Classicist character. Standing out vividly against the greenish walls are white bas-reliefs; the panels of the doors are covered by white carved ornamental compositions with painted insets in the form of cameos. The vaulted ceiling is covered with monochrome painting in the grisaille technique. On a mahogany writing desk in the Study stands an ormolu candelabrum executed in 1783 in St Petersburg from a drawing by Cameron. The amaranth armchairs and the ormolu chandelier with faceted crystal were created in the early nineteenth century.

Later the Studies housed the private library of Yelizaveta Alexeyevna. The collection of the Empress's favourite books and numerous sheets of music were preserved in special cases. Her harp and guitar were also kept here. It was supposed that Alexander I's wife would live in the part of the Small Enfilade, while the Emperor occupied the next rooms. The children of Alexander and Yelizaveta died at an early age and their family relations took an unfavourable turn, so they had no joint rooms in the palace and each of them occupied separate apartments.

140

142

THE MAIN (MARBLE) STUDY OF EMPEROR ALEXANDER I

The private apartments of Alexander II were situated on the site of the private apartments of the Small Enfilade which had been decorated by Bartolomeo Francesco Rastrelli for Elizabeth Petrovna. In 1817 Vasily Stasov created here a whole number of interiors in the style of Late Classicism, from which the Oval Lobby, the Vaulted Passage Room and the Main (Marble) Study have been reconstructed by now. These rooms suffered from fire in 1820 and Stasov himself recreated them in 1822. Alexander I preferred to stay in these rooms although in the last year of Catherine II's life a palace had been built specially for him.

The Main (Marble) Study of Emperor Alexander I combines an imposing architectural solution with a strict simplicity in the decoration of the walls and the ceiling, which are faced with pale pink artificial marble and decorated with painting in the grisaille technique. The entrance to the study is designed as a deep exedra or niche separated from the main volume by Ionic columns of a greenish colour. Similar columns flank the marble fireplace in the centre of the opposite wall. The lunettes under the vault of the ceiling feature scenes from a myth about Cupid and Psyche. The study is provided with a furniture set of Persian walnut executed to Stasov's design by the well-known St Petersburg cabinet-maker Andrei Tour.

142, 144. The Main (Marble) Study of Emperor Alexander I

143. Clock: *Julius Caesar*. 1812–17. By M.-L. Feshcher, Paris. Bronze, marble, malachite

143

THE MARBLE (STASOV'S) STAIRCASE
CHURCH OF THE RESURRECTION
THE CHURCH ANTEROOM

The Marble (Stasov) Staircase was constructed between 1843 and 1846 by the architect Vasily Stasov (hence its present-day name) on the site of the old round staircase. On either side of the staircase hang paintings by French and Italian artists of the seventeenth and eighteenth centuries. Originally the staircase was named the Church Staircase as it was situated next to the hall leading to the home church.

The Church of the Resurrection was built in 1745–48 by Rastrelli with a contribution by Alexei Kvasov and Savva Chevakinsky. Grand Duke Nikolai Pavlovich was baptized here. It was also in this palatial church that the coffin with the body of Emperor Alexander I who died at Taganrog was installed.

People used to wait for the beginning of the service in the spacious, richly decorated Church Anteroom designed by Vasily Stasov in the 1840s. This interior is situated between the Church and the vestibule of the ground floor.

145. The Marble (Stasov's) Staircase

146. The Church Anteroom

147. Church of the Resurrection. View of the Holy Doors

149

THE CATHERINE PARK

In 1728, Tsarskoye Selo became the property of Elizabeth Petrovna following a decree issued by Peter the Great. Before ascending to the throne, she often came here to hunt and oversee the cultivation of the orchards on the estate. When Empress Elizabeth decided to create a little Versailles in Tsarskoye Selo, she accorded Bartolomeo Francesco Rastrelli complete artistic freedom. He remodelled the main features of the park and palace ensemble for Elizabeth, although they are historically known as the Catherine Park and Catherine Palace respectively.

Rastrelli perfected the regular park that had been planned earlier, stretching out from the east façade of the Catherine Palace. From water, trees, marble and stone he produced a true ode to the eighteenth century. As if by magic, he conjured up mirror ponds, parterre flowerbeds and intricate mazes in which marble sculptures created by Italians charm us with their sensual beauty. The attractive arrangement of alleys laid out in front of the Catherine Palace was ideally suited to unhurried strolls and ceremonial processions. The architect included into his composition two garden pavilions: the Hermitage and the Grotto.

←
148. A bird's-eye view of the Catherine Palace

149. The Cameron Gallery.
1784–87. Architect: Charles Cameron

150. The Cameron Ramp. Decorative vase.
1828. Designed by Vasily Stasov. Bronze

151. The Old Garden. Parterre

152. The Cameron Gallery. Main Staircase

153

154

The oldest part of the Catherine Park is the garden, which stretches out before the east façade of the Catherine Palace. Its avenues are lined with marble sculptures. Only a small number of the statues and busts that were to be found here in the eighteenth and nineteenth centuries have survived to this day. Several of them bear inscriptions. The names of masters of the Venetian school at the turn of the eighteenth century – Pietro Baratta, Antonio Tarsia and Giovanni Bonazza – are to be seen on the pedestals. Works by these sculptors also grace the Summer Garden in Petersburg. It was Baratta who created one of the best statues in the garden,

153. The Old Garden. Decorative sculptures.
17th–18th century. Marble

154. View of the Cameron Gallery from the park

155. The Cameron Ramp. 1792–94. Architect: Charles Cameron

156. The Cameron Gallery. View of the colonnade

155

156

157

157. The Agate Rooms. The Great Hall

158. The Agate Rooms. The Great Hall. Etienne Maurice
Falconet. *Cupid Menacing with His Finger*. 1758. Marble

159. View of the Agate Rooms from the Hanging Garden.
1784–87. Architect: Charles Cameron

160. The Agate Rooms. The Agate Study. Ceiling painting

158

the representation of Galatea. This small statue was conceived as the centrepiece of a fountain.

In the 1770s–'80s, buildings that now constitute stylish monuments to Russian Classicism were also erected in the Catherine Park. Catherine the Great once described the work of Charles Cameron in one of her letters: "Now I have got my hands on the master Cameron, a Scotsman by birth, a Jacobin by profession and a great draughtsman, who is full of knowledge of the ancients and is renowned for his book on ancient bathhouses. Here in Tsarskoye Selo we are creating a terraced garden with bathhouses below and a gallery above. It will be charming!" It was not the interiors that brought Cameron the fame he deserved, but the splendid architectural edifices that he built, of which there are several in Tsarskoye Selo. The largest and most illustrious of these is the Cameron Gallery, named after its designer.

The Gallery and the adjoining Agate Rooms, Cold Bath, Hanging Garden and Ramp make up a harmonious "Greco-Roman rhapsody". Indeed, this architectural composition, which comprises several buildings created to serve a variety of functions, is inspiring for its grandeur, originality and the boldness of its design.

The Cameron Gallery created by Cameron, an outstanding interpreter of ancient motifs, is called an architectural "poem" in the spirit of Classicism. Pushkin recalls it a "huge hall" soaring towards clouds and dominating the Catherine Gardens. The Cameron Gallery, intended for meditation, promenades, social intercourse and contemplation of the splendid landscape that stretches out on all sides, plays an important part in the ensemble. The architect chose a truly appropriate spot for it on the slope of the hill leading down to the Great Pond.

The ground floor of the Gallery is made of massive stone blocks. Here were the living quarters for courtiers. The bright, glass-faced hall on the first floor, surrounded on all sides by a colonnade, seems still lighter and airier in comparison to the solid ground floor. The magnificent outer staircase with its elegantly curving flight of steps is a wonderful architectural creation in its own right. The Gallery is decorated with 54 busts of philosophers, poets, emperors, military leaders, gods and heroes of antiquity. The only contemporary of Cameron's whose likeness is included in this series is Mikhail Lomonosov.

161. The Cameron Gallery. View from above

162. The Cameron Gallery. The Main Staircase. *Hercules.* 1786. Copy from an antique original. Cast after the model of Fiodor Gordeyev. Bronze

162

163

The Ramp installed by Cameron serves as an organic link between the architectural ensemble and the surrounding landscaped gardens. It also represents one of Cameron's artistic triumphs. The architect treated it in the manner of ancient cyclopean structures like aqueducts, open waterways of Ancient Rome. The decor of the walls is eye-catching: enormous masks cut from local limestone adorn the keystones of the arches. Amongst the heroes of ancient mythology to be seen here are Mercury, Pan, Silenus, Neptune and

163. View of the Agate Rooms Pavilion from the Ladies-in-Waiting Garden

164. View of the Ramp from the Cameron Gallery

165. The Private Garden. The Pergola

166. The Private Garden. *Dancer*. Early 19th century. Copy from the original by Antonio Canova. Marble

167. The Private Garden. *Nymph*. 1860s. Sculptor: Parmen Zabello. Marble

164

165

166

167

169

168. The Upper Bath Pavilion.
Ceiling painting and murals
(copies of the paintings
of the Neron Domus Aureus).
Mid-19th century.
By Alexei Belsky according
the watercolours of Franciszek
Smuglewicz

169, 170. The Upper Bath
Pavilion. 1777–79.
Architect: Ilya Neyelov

171. The Upper Bath Pavilion.
Detail of the interior

168

others. The powerful, gradually descending arches divided by semicircular supports-columns bear the gently sloping descent which is linked to the Ramp Avenue. The composition of the Ramp was completed with bronze statues in 1794. Later, by order of Paul I, they were moved to Pavlovsk, and in 1828 decorative wrought iron bowls reminiscent of ancient lamps were installed to replace them (they are attributed to Stasov). The Ramp forms an effective perspective along the middle axis and produces an impression of a complex of triumphal arches from the side.

In 1780–87 Charles Cameron erected the building of the Cold Baths as a single ensemble with the Gallery. The volume and façades of the Cold Baths appear from the side of the gallery as a small pavilion, but from the side of the park it looks like a massive structure. The heavily rusticated fronts of the Cold Baths are decorated with bronze and stone statues. The two-storey building is angled towards the sun just as Roman thermal baths were. On the lower floor are the Cold

172

173

Baths for which Cameron devised a special plumbing system. The interiors of the upper floor are called the Agate Rooms. They are faced with plaques of coloured stone, mainly marble and jasper of various types and shades. The noble colours of natural stones determine the unique designs of the Amber, Agate and Small Studies, Great Oval Hall, staircase, testifying to the exclusive taste of the architect, sculptors and stone carvers who created this unique ensemble.

"Travelling to Tsarskoye with a small retinue, Catherine divided her time between affairs of state and all manner of amusements. Every day she would take a walk in the park in the company of the knights and maids of the court… Of all the country residences, Catherine's favourite was Tsarskoye Selo. From 1763 onwards, with the exception of 2 or 3 years, she lived in Tsarskoye Selo in spring and spent practically all summer here, leaving in the autumn when the weather grew cold. It is here that she celebrated almost every one of her birthdays, and from here that she set out on her ceremonial journey to Petersburg on 28 June 1763 after the coronation in Moscow" (Sergei Vilchkovsky).

Besides the palace and the Cameron Gallery, the Catherine Park contains a number of small pavilions, which serve various purposes. Often located on the shores of a pond or lake, they are magically reflected in the still surface of the waters.

Rastrelli endowed the Hermitage Pavilion with such a decorative majesty that it began to resemble a miniature palace. With her insatiable taste for novel amusements, Elizabeth was particularly fond of dining with her courtiers in this pavilion. Traditionally, the lower storey of the Hermitage had mechanisms which were used to lift laid tables for meals held in the Central Hall of the upper floor. As a rule the procedure began in the very heat of a ball. The floors would suddenly open and exquisite dishes would appear from below to the guests' pleasant surprise.

172. The Hermitage Pavilion.
Detail of the façade

173. The Hermitage Pavilion. 1749–54.
Architect: Bartolomeo Francesco Rastrelli

174. A bird's eye-view of the Hermitage

175

176

177

178

175. The Hermitage Pavilion.
The Main Hall

176. The Hermitage Pavilion.
The Eastern Study. Ceiling painting

177. The Hermitage Pavilion.
The Eastern Gallery.
Overdoor decoration

178. The Hermitage Pavilion.
The Eastern Gallery. Detail of carved
decoration

179. The Hermitage Pavilion.
The Eastern Study. Door

→

180. The Hermitage Pavilion.
The Main Hall. Ceiling painting
The Feast of Gods

→

181. The Hermitage Pavilion.
The Main Hall. Detail of carved
decoration

→

182. The Hermitage Pavilion.
The Main Hall. Detail of the inlaid
parquet floor

183

184

The Grotto Pavilion or Morning Room built by Rastrelli on the bank of the Great Pond was used for recreation during boating parties. The pavilion's location and designation determined its fairy-tale moulded decor with sea monsters, dolphins and sea-shells. The Grotto blends beautifully with the panorama of the Great Pond. It is a characteristic example of the small architectural structures that adorn the horizons of the park at Tsarskoye Selo. Unlike the emphatically decorative pavilions in the Baroque style, Classicist architects lent to garden structures geometrically clear-cut shapes accentuated by relief insets. Such is the Upper Bath Pavilion built in the 1770s by the architect Ilya Neyelov.

183. The Granite Terrace. Statues – copies from antique originals. 1851. By Johann Hamburger. Galvanoplastic

184. The Granite Terrace. 1809–10. Architect: Luigi Rusca

185. Parterre in front of the Granite Terrace

In 1772–74, the architect Vasily Neyelov erected a remarkable bridge over the Great Pond. It was initially referred to as the Siberian Marble Gallery, since its component parts were prepared in Ekaterinburg from marble mined in the Urals and delivered to Tsarskoye Selo, where they were assembled over a period of two years. The dark water of the pond reflects and replicates the precise arrangement of the columns. It subsequently came to be known as the Palladian Bridge in honour of the famous Italian architect and theoretician, Andrea Palladio.

186. The Grotto Pavilion (Morning Room). 1749–61. Architect: Bartolomeo Francesco Rastrelli

187. Palladian Bridge (Siberian, Marble Gallery). 1772–74. Architect: Vasily Neyelov

Under Catherine the Great, the vast park with an area of 100.5 hectares became a "pantheon of Russian greatness". The unique ensemble of monuments, which includes the Chesme Column and the Column of Morea, the Kagul Obelisk and the Crimean Column, commemorates the Turkish campaigns of the 1760s and '70s, the crowning glory of the Russian forces.

The most famous monument to Catherine the Great, the Chesme Rostral Column, soars on a small island of the Great Pond. It was erected to a design by Antonio Rinaldi in 1774–76 to commemorate the victory of the Russian squadron over eet in Chesme Bay in the Aegean Sea in 1770.

188. The Chesme (Orlov) Column.
Eagle Trampling the Crescent. 1770s.
Sculptor: Ivan Schwarz. Bronze

189. The Chesme (Orlov) Column. 1774–76.
Architect: Antonio Rinaldi

190. Granite landing-stage
on the bank of the Great Pond

191. The "Hall-on-the-Island". 1817–19.
Architects: Vasily Stasov and Piotr Neyelov

193

194

195

196

In 2010 work on the restoration of the Concert Hall, a masterpiece of Classicism, has been completed. Giacomo Quarenghi built the pavilion for Catherine the Great and decorated its western front with an open rotunda of ten columns. Highly valuable is the mosaic floor of the central interior. Datable from the late second and early third centuries A.D. and brought from Rome in 1784, it depicts a scene of the rape of Europe. The ceiling paintings in the pavilion were executed by the artists G. Valesini, I. Bogdanov, I. Scotti, F. Danilov and I. Christ.

←
192. Panoramic view of the Catherine Park. In the centre, the Great Lake

193. The Concert Hall. 1780s. Architect: Giacomo Quarenghi

194, 196. The Concert Hall Pavilion. Floor mosaics in the Great Hall. Late 2nd – early 3rd century A.D. Rome. Marble

195. The Concert Hall. The Great Hall

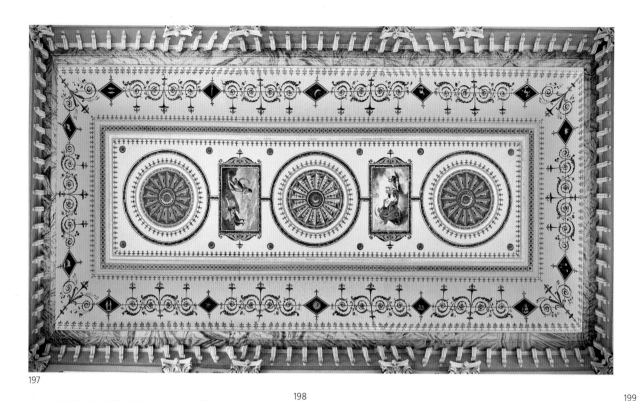

197

The landscaped section of the Catherine Park is situated around the Great Pond. A number of unique park pavilions are connected with it, among which the Turkish Bath reminiscent of a miniature mosque. It was designed by Hippolyto Monighetti in 1850–52. Built in honour of Russia's victory over the Turks in the war of 1828–29 the pavilion stands on the southwest shore of the pond. Having given his brainchild

197. The Concert Hall Pavilion.
Ceiling painting in the Great Hall

198. The Concert Hall. The Great Hall.
Detail of the interior

199. The Concert Hall Pavilion.
View of the Great Hall from the gallery

200. The Concert Hall Pavilion.
Ceiling painting in the gallery

201. The Concert Hall Pavilion.
Floor mosaics in the gallery. Late 1st –
early 2nd century A.D. Rome. Marble

200

201

203

the external appearance of a mosque with three-tiered minarets, the architect then embellished the interior with genuine articles of Eastern applied art, namely marble slabs taken from fountains and carved with verses in Arabic.

From the 1770s onwards, a preoccupation with "historical" styles such as the Gothic and, in particular, the Oriental "Turkic" and "Chinoiserie" styles, became apparent in the architecture within the gardens. On the shore of the Great Pond, for example, the Admiralty ensemble, consisting of three buildings, was created. The name is derived from the fact that the central structure was used as a boathouse. Its round turret and the arrow slits cut into the brick walls are a testimony to the English Gothic style.

Tsarskoye Selo is not simply dear to Russians because it was one of the imperial country residences for many years. This place is also inseparably linked to the name of the great Russian poet Alexander Pushkin, who studied at the Lyceum (now a branch of the Pushkin Museum) and continued to visit the village at various times throughout his life. Even people who have not been to Tsarskoye Selo can clearly picture its various features and get a feel for their charms when reading the poet's verses. It seems that the writer extols every inch of the park, including the renowned *Milkmaid Fountain, or the Girl with a Pitcher* (1816, sculptor Pavel Sokolov), which was built over the only natural spring in the park. The fountain later on has been celebrated by poets. It is covered by a granite boulder crowned with the bronze figure of a young girl crying over the broken pitcher.

←

202. The Admiralty ("Holland"). 1773–77. Architect: Vasily Neyelov

203. The Turkish Bath Pavilion. 1850–52. Architect: Hippolyto Monighetti

204–207. The Turkish Bath Pavilion . Details of the interior

204

205

206

208

a Pushkin museum. The poet lived at the *dacha* together with his young wife Natalia Goncharova in 1831.

It is the Lyceum that evokes especially vivid associations connected with the poet's youth spent at Tsarskoye Selo. In 1811 the former palatial wing, linked in 1789–91 with the Great Palace by a gallery, was given to the newly founded privileged educational establishment named the Lyceum. Here Alexander Pushkin studied between 1811 and 1817. Pushkin devoted to the Lyceum and Tsarskoye Selo, where "the Muse appeared" to him for the first time, a number of beautiful verses.

On 8 January 1815 in the Assembly Hall of the Lyceum, one of the most important events in the life of Pushkin and the history of Russian poetry took place. Eminent guests, including the outstanding eighteenth-century Russian poet Gavriil Derzhavin, were invited to attend the examinations at the Lyceum, during which the young Pushkin read a poem that he had composed

208. The Kagul Obelisk. 1771–72. Architect: Antonio Rinaldi

209. Metal Bridge (1780s, architect: Giacomo Quarenghi), The Red (Turkish) Cascade and the Pudost Bridge

210. Fountain: *The Milkmaid, or the Girl with a Pitcher*. 1816. Sculptor: Pavel Sokolov

209

Tsarskoye Selo, which Pushkin associated in his verses with the idea of home-land, became the holy land of Russian poetry for subsequent generations. There are many buildings in Tsarskoye Selo connected with Pushkin's life – the house of Ludwig Wilhelm Tepper de Ferguson, a music teacher in the Lyceum, and the mansion of Vasily Malinovsky and Yegor Engelgardt, its first directors, the house of the writer and historian Nikolai Karamzin, and the famous Kitayeva's *dacha* which now houses

211

212

specially for the occasion, entitled "Recollections of Tsarskoye Selo". Many years later the poet wrote: "I only saw Derzhavin once, but I will never forget it… He dozed right up until the Russian literature examination, at which point he was completely transformed… At last, my name was called… I cannot describe the state I was in: when I got to the part where I refer to Derzhavin, my voice turned into an adolescent squeak and my heart began to pound with intoxicating delight… I do not recall how I finished the recital; I do not remember where I ran off to. Derzhavin was enraptured, he wanted to embrace me. They looked for me, but they could not find me." That is how Pushkin won his first poetic acclaim. He was fifteen years old.

To commemorate the Lyceum years of Pushkin in honour of the centenary of the poet's birth, on 2 May

211. The Ruin Tower. 1771–73. Architect: Yury Velten

212. Metal Bridge. 1784. Architect: Giacomo Quarenghi

213. The Pyramid. 1770–73. Architect: Vasily Neyelov

214. Triumphal gate: *To My Dear Comrades-in-Arms.* 1817. Architect: Adam Menelaws

213

214

215

216

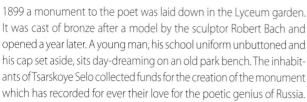

1899 a monument to the poet was laid down in the Lyceum garden. It was cast of bronze after a model by the sculptor Robert Bach and opened a year later. A young man, his school uniform unbuttoned and his cap set aside, sits day-dreaming on an old park bench. The inhabitants of Tsarskoye Selo collected funds for the creation of the monument which has recorded for ever their love for the poetic genius of Russia.

The Golden Gate decorates the main entrance to the Catherine Palace. Behind it, in keeping with the tradition of eighteenth-century architecture, is the formal courtyard arranged in front of the main west façade of the palace adorned with semicircular service wings. In 1752–56 Rastrelli stylistically united the service blocks with the Baroque courtyard. Put up in the gaps between them were fences and gates with pylons. The graphic silhouette of the forged frame is enhanced and completed by a variety of elaborate gilded scrolls, garlands, sea-shells, feathers and stars.

The main gate is crowned with the Imperial coat of arms, the gilded double-headed eagle, which emphasizes the designation of Tsarskoye Selo as a royal residence.

217

218

219

215. Statue of Pushkin in the garden of the Lyceum.
1900. Sculptor: Robert Bach

216. The Catherine Palace church and the Lyceum

217. The Lyceum. Great Hall. 1811. Architect: Vasily Stasov

218. Ilya Repin. *Pushkin at the Lyceum Examination
in Tsarskoye Selo on 8 January 1815*. 1911

219. The Lyceum. Pushkin's room

→

220. Railings of the gate of the Catherine Palace

221

THE ALEXANDER PALACE
THE ALEXANDER PARK

Beyond the bounds of the main estate at Tsarskoye Selo lies another famous park. The Alexander Park was laid in the early nineteenth century and combines regular gardens and landscaped features. The design of the palace blends subtly with the surrounding landscape so that the building becomes an integral part of the natural setting rather than the dominant feature. The Alexander Palace largely owes its rare magnificence to the double colonnade uniting the extending parts of the north front, with a happily found rhythm of the "movement" of slender shafts crowned by the capitals of the Corinthian order.

During the reign of Nicholas I it became the favourite residence of the Emperor's family who lived in Alexander Palace from the early spring till the end of May and after a short stay at Krasnoye Selo during manoeuvres returned to the Alexander Palace to spend their time there until the late autumn.

Nicholas I had some rooms and the park redesigned in the then fashionable Romantic manner. Later Emperor Alexander III had his apartments in the right-hand wing of the palace.

The palace interiors suffered during the war. In the summer of 1997, a permanent exhibition was opened in the left wing of the building. Today, certain

221. The Alexander Palace. 1792–96.
Architect: Giacomo Quarenghi

222. The Rotunda

223. The Portrait Hall

224

225

elements of the Reception Room, Nicholas II's New Study and Al-exandra Fiodorovna's Corner Drawing Room have been recreated and provide a fascinating backdrop to the exhibitions of historical costumes, weapons and objects of applied art to be found within their walls. In Nicholas II's beautifully preserved Study, where the working environment of the last Russian Emperor has been recreated, hangs a portrait of Nicholas II's father painted by the great Russian artist, Valentin Serov. In the children's quarters, visitors can see dresses once worn by the grand princesses and outfits and toys belonging to the Tsarevich Alexei.

In 1910–12 Vladimir Pokrovsky and Stepan Krichinsky erected for Nicholas II near the Alexander Palace the Cathedral of the Fiodor-ovskaya Icon of the Mother of God which became the focal centre of the closed royal town. Its architecture reproduced the imagery and decorative motifs of ancient Russian Orthodox churches.

227

224. Vladimir Makovsky.
Portrait of Nicholas II

225. Nikolai Bodarevsky.
Empress Alexandra Fiodorovna. 1907

226. The Corner Drawing Room
of Empress Alexandra Fiodorovna

227. Anonymous artist.
Portrait of Tsarevich Alexis. 1910

228. Emperor Nicholas II and his family. 1904.
Photograph

229. Nicholas II's New Study

228

226

229

The Chinoiserie style found its embodiment at Tsarskoye Selo in a number of bridges in the Catherine Park and, in particular, in the ensemble known as the Chinese Village put up on the orders of Catherine the Great at the border of the Catherine and Alexander Parks. The latter comprises ten houses with intricate lines and decorative curved roofs. In the late nineteenth century the interior design of the cottages was changed to house the guests of the imperial family. Every pavillion was furnished with a bed, a small table, a wardrobe, a chest of drawers, a writing desk. It was equipped with tea- and coffee services (samovar included). Every cottage overlooked a small garden.

Situated in the Alexander Park, this complex is linked to the Catherine Park by two bridges. One of these is the Great Caprice, which constitutes a unique work of park architecture.

230. Large Chinese Bridge. 1780s.
Architect: Charles Cameron

231. Dragon Bridge. 1785.
Architect: Charles Cameron

232. The Creaking Pavilion. 1778–86.
Architect: Yury Velten

233

234

235

The bridge is crowned with an elegant pagoda in which the European form of the octagonal rotunda is combined with an Eastern-style upturned roof. The second is the Cross Bridge, a fascinating structure consisting of two intersecting spans. On the bridge itself stands an octagonal pavilion with a curved roof, which sports an ornamental spike topped with a sphere.

The Creaking Pavilion was erected nearby to the design of Yury Velten. This pavilion crowned with weather-vanes attracted visitors' attention primarily by its unusual chinoiserie decoration.

A complex of "Chinese amusements" was increased by the construction of a group of the so-called Chinese Bridges created in the late 1770s and early 1780s. Besides the Cross Bridge, there are four of them – the Dragon Bridge, two iron Chinese bridges and the Large Stone Bridge.

233. Small Chinese Bridge. 1781–82.
Architect: Charles Cameron

234. Cross Bridge. 1776–79.
Architects: Vasily and Ilya Neyelov

→

235, 237, 238. The Chinese Village.
1782–98, architects: Antonio Rinaldi, Vasily Neyelov and Charles Cameron; 1817–22, architect: Vasily Stasov

236. The Great Caprice. 1772–74. Architect: Vasily Neyelov

240

241

242

In 1827 Menelaws erected the White Tower intended for the sons of Emperor Nicholas I – Grand Dukes Alexander, Konstantin, Nikolai and Mikhail, – who studied military art in the Alexander Park. Pained white, the structure consisted of several tiers and was crowned by a crenellated parapet, while on the fronts in niches were set up cast-iron figures of knights. The building was encircled by the walls of a bastion and a moat filled with water. The 1990s saw a start of the architectural restoration of the monument that enabled to bring back its former architectural appearance.

The architectural wonders of Tsarskoye Selo are not only to be seen in the grounds of the parks, but also in the town. On the road that runs alongside the Alexander Park, the Egyptian Gates, designed by Menelaws, were erected in 1827–30. The gateposts that flank the arch resemble truncated pyramids. They are decorated with rows of reliefs showing genuine Egyptian characters. The stylised stems of the sacred Egyptian flower, the lotus, are entwined in the metal grille. These gates formed the main entrance to the town from the Petersburg side.

239. The Chapel Tower. 1825–28. Architect: Adam Menelaws

240. The White Tower. 1826. Architect: Adam Menelaws

241. The Arsenal. 1816–34. Architect: Adam Menelaws

242. View of the Upper Pond and the Creaking Pavilion (1776–86, architect: Yury Velten)

→

243. The Catherine Palace and the main courtyard

TSARSKOYE SELO

Text: Galina Khodasevich, Natalia Popova, Abram Raskin

Translation: Valery Fateyev

Photographs: Leonid Bogdanov, Sergei Chistobayev, Pavel Demidov, Vladimir Denisov, Valery Gordt, Denis Lazarev, Boris Manushin, Vladimir Melnikov, Alexander Minin, Alexander Petrosian, Sergei Podmiotin, Nikolai Rakhmanov, Viktor Savik, Vladimir Shlakan, Yevgeny Siniaver, Irina Tereshenkova, Oleg Trubsky, Vasily Vorontsov

Editors: Irina Kharitonova and Irina Lvova

Computer layout: Svetlana Bashun

Colour correction: Viacheslav Bykovsky, Vladimir Kniazev, Alexander Miagkov

Revised and enlarged edition

Торговый дом «Медный всадник»
www.mvsadnik.ru
Тел./факс (812) 320-91-35

Изготовитель ООО «Новатор»
Россия, 194156, Санкт-Петербург, пр. Энгельса, д. 27

Формат бумаги 60 x 90 ⅛. Бумага мелованная, печать офсетная